4 A.M. THOUGHTS

JORDAN JURKOWSKI

DoctorZed
Publishing
www.doctorzed.com

ISBN: 978-0-6455442-9-9 (sc)
ISBN: 978-0-6455072-0-1 (ebk)

First published by DoctorZed Publishing, 2022

DoctorZed Publishing books may be ordered through booksellers or by contacting:

DoctorZed Publishing
IDAHO
10 Vista Ave
Skye, South Australia 5072
www.doctorzed.com
orders@doctorzed.com

Printed in Australia, UK, and USA

rev. date 07/07/2022

CONTENTS

This Book Is For

For Erica – My darling wife. For supporting this book happening and all my dreams. For helping edit this book! Your hard work is appreciated.

For Mum who has helped edit this book! Your hard work is appreciated.

For Dad, Vernon, Vanessa, Ryan, Isabel, Troy, Amber, Phoebe & Blayke – for being the best family ever!

For Dziadek, may you rest in peace.

For Grandad, now we both have a book each. Rest in peace.

"Sic Parvis Magna"

WHY I WROTE THIS BOOK

I have written this book to showcase my poems and journal thoughts. I have always loved the art for writing and writing this book is an accomplishment for my writing journey as well as my creative one.

This book features subjects such as death, love, loss, family, depression, anxiety, existentialism and inner peace. My writing reflects these times and I have tried to be as real as possible.

I wrote this book when I was up, alone in the early hours of the morning, hence the title, 4 A.M. Thoughts

TRIBUTES

HELLO YOU BEAUTIFUL PEOPLE

"HELLO YOU BEAUTIFUL PEOPLE"
Warming us with your classic greeting,
I can still hear the way your voice sounded
and the way you smiled
Every meeting and every Polish meal that
you cooked, and we were eating
I think back of fondly and say I am proud to
be your grandchild
I remember so many things, so many
Sometimes I still listen for your laughs but
I'm not hearing any

When I was young, at yours and Nanna's
house I would sleep
You read me bedtime stories and even the
bible until you didn't hear me peep
I remember just lying-in bed
You sat on a chair besides, and I would
admire you as you read
That was way back when I had tiny sleepy
eyes and ears
And I'm still talking about it
after all these years
What about all those visits,
for lunch or dinner?
More eating less talking, we'd leave looking
the opposite of thinner
You'd be on the BBQ and we would come out
and help cook
You were like a real-life human cookbook
I think you are behind my coffee and
dark chocolate addiction
You gave me my first sips, no word of fiction

Or all the Christmas mornings, you'd put on
a feast
And if we couldn't eat it all, the family was
together at least
You always threw your coffee grounds
on the grass
You always were interested in our schooling
and hoped we would pass
You loved, loved, loved a good game of chess
I have one regret I guess
If I could go back, every time you would ask
to play, I would say "No" less and more "Yes"
You would get so eager over an exciting
game, making your opponent look
quite weak
Your mind and tactics in their peak
When I was learning to drive, you would
always say
"Don't rush, take your time" and I remember
it till this day
When the Alzheimer's hit

You hit back and didn't back down one bit
When we visited in the home, you would love
seeing us and we loved seeing you
You were forgetting things, but there was still
a lot you knew
You always remembered us and gifted us
your warm smile
You always would sit and talk a while
When I told you, I got into Uni,
your eyes lit up
You told me it was wonderful; it was clear
you had your spirit up
Growing up, hearing about your hard life and
time in the army and seeing pictures with all
those muscles atop those bones
I thought you were really Indiana Jones!
You were a boy lost; a man found
You pushed on and never fell to the ground
I'd like to think that whenever your life
seemed a mess
Or there was lots of stress
You would shrug and say
"It's one big game of chess"

That or yetz yetz
Oh Dziadek, if only you could see what I've become...
I like to think you can still see; it makes it less glum
I have met the best girl ever; I think you'd like her... She plays chess too sometimes...
I graduated Uni
I am now married
(wish you were at the wedding)
I am buying a house
I have a good job
All these things I hope you can see atop of your cloud
I really do hope that you are proud
And as the end of my long and successful life eventually awaits
"HELLO YOU BEAUTIFUL PEOPLE"
That's what I expect to hear as I walk through the pearly gates.

GOOD MOURNING

Good morning. The sun has risen!
And with it, an end to their self-made prison
I hope your spirit has reached the sky
If you're looking down, I'd imagine a sparkle
in your eye
I know, It's quite the sight!
Finally, an end to that dark, dark night
And it's all your doing
All those years of emotions stewing
For what? I'm uncertain, as I was just a
spectator viewing
A distant memory for all – bad memories
fade
so good new ones can be made

But you, you knew how to bring them back
You knew it had to be the right time or plans
would go off track
Typical Grandad, so particular – one of the
things your family misses
Along with your voice, your stories, games,
puzzles and quizzes
When I get anxious and depressed like you
did and when my voice starts to shake and
mumble
I will think of my Grandad, a true gentleman
and oh so humble
A thinker, always creative and critical
I would swear to God but can't get any more
biblical
I miss the visits most of all
That's when the tears start to fall
I would approach the table where he sat,
wearing Green Bay
He'd tell a few jokes – the clean way
To hell with small-talk, there was purpose in
the words he'd say

So, I felt honoured when he wanted
my brother and I to work with him on a
screenplay
Him and I shared information in a keen play
We – your wife, children, grandchildren and
great grandchildren – will miss you dearly
In your death, you brought your family
together again, it's seen so clearly
So yes, we lost You, Gerald, the Wise
That should now be your dub
But it's a blessing in disguise
There's the rub!
You lifted the dark clouds off your family,
clearing a path for sunny days and reunited
them – good mourning.
You're an inspiration, Grandad. I hope to
make you proud as a fellow writer.

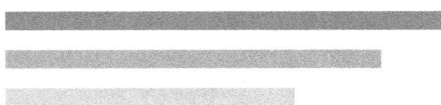

THERE'S THE RUB

For a long time, I thought I was done with writing. No more good ideas, no more energy, no more caring. That was true, for the most part, up until I found your transcripts. Something told me to read through them. Something drew me into them. I took them, read them and put them in my nerd room. Fast forward two weeks later, the 17th March, Saint Patricks Day AKA your birthday. You would have been 83. I thought of you all day that day. I took out your light green book sporting a wide-eyed owl on the front. I still cannot believe you published your own book. A picture of you fell out of the front page. It was from your funeral. As the picture landed on the table, it was almost as if we made eye contact for a split second. Weird, I know. As soon as I made eye contact, I opened your book up again. Read through it. I could feel something. Powerful. A burning in my chest. Something had been reignited inside me. I looked at your picture again; it was then I realised…I need to write my own book too. Like you. The burning I felt in my chest was a fire, a spark of inspiration. Your eyes in that tiny little memorial card picture told me to keep writing, to write a book. Now, your book sits in my nerd room where I can see it in plain view, as a reminder of what you accomplished and of what I can accomplish too. That is how I went from giving up on writing and found my way back to it…as you would say…there's the rub! Holy Mackerel!

DEATH

WALK AMONGST
THE SLEEP

*Walk amongst the sleep, their bodies now
resting in the ground
As I walk, nightmares creep over me, I can
hear the sounds
Howling, moaning, whispering in my ear
There is no oxygen to breathe in, only fear
Skin and bone have moved on, leaving only
voices of despair
They still have stories to tell us, be aware
"Died 1945, aged 21; died 1840, aged 55;
died 2010, aged 85; died 1950, aged 1 day"
There's a lesson here
And now I'm sure it's clear*

When you leave this life make sure you're
exhausted
Experience all you can with an open mind
Live a life well defined
In other words, live a life with lots of meaning
A full life, make a reality out of your
dreaming
Before time is up and it ends
Before you're struggling for one last breath
and your soul ascends
Because then you can stand face-to-face
with death and feel no threat
For you will have no regret
Walk amongst the sleep and I thank them for
reaching out
Triumphant successes and failures alike
As I listen close, those howls, nightmares,
whispers, turn into life lessons
As I'm chasing ghosts, I'd like to make a toast
Thank you.

TELL ME (VILLANELLE POEM)

Tell me Uncle Tony, was it hard?
So many things now seem changed
We are all now forever scarred
Your choice left my heart charred
We were still in contact, yet estranged
Tell me Uncle Tony, was it hard?
Maybe it wasn't. Did you lose your guard?
The day you got the gun your fate
was arranged
Maybe you were the one who was scarred
Now look, suicide in a lonely yard
One act, now your soul is exchanged

Tell me Uncle Tony, was it hard?
We lost an uncle because your mind was marred
The feeling of not being able to help you, ranged
Your memory shouldn't be associated with being scarred
This is the hand we have been dealt and you played your card
Maybe God has dealt them in ways utterly deranged
Tell me Uncle Tony, was it hard?
We are all now forever scarred.

LIFE

Why is the World Your Oyster?

*Why is the world my oyster? The thought is
disappointing
Oysters smell horrible, pungent and fishy
Sometimes they leave us pearls, but pearls
can be stolen with guns pointing
Oysters may be hard on the outer, but inside
are weak and squishy
Oysters are hard to open, yet so unrewarding
Oyster shells are rough and uneasy to hold
Determining an oyster to be good or off is a
risk in which some cannot be affording
Upon opening it after hard work, one will
find that it is wet and cold*

Oysters give the ability to be our own pearls
but at what cost?
Everything is now valued from low to high
Forget it if your pearl is not smooth, round or
glossed
If your pearl isn't up to par, kiss your value
goodbye
So, tell me, why would I want an oyster to
explore?
We create our own opportunities and worlds,
that's what imagination is for.

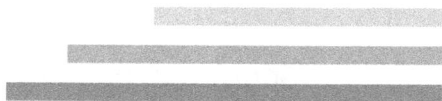

Shoes/Walks of Life (Free-Verse)

"What is it like in your shoes?"

I don't even know what shoes I have.
Does the pair I have fit me?
Sometimes they're too tight. How can I
make room?
Sometimes they're too loose. How can I
fill them?
They trip me up. Make me stumble.
They help me to hit the ground running.
Sometimes it feels like I have no shoes on.

The feeling of no shoes –
I get lost as to what path I can walk.
Sometimes my shoes break,
making change a necessity.
New shoes come at a cost in which some
cannot afford.
Sometimes others do not like my shoes
and start to judge.
Sometimes others like my shoes
and envy them.
Sometimes I judge and envy the shoes
of others.
Sometimes my shoes get messy.
I guess I'm lucky
to be in shoes in the first place.
Never start your shoes off on the wrong foot.
Sometimes shoes cannot support our weight.
Supporting weight – take a load off, forge
new shoes, press on.
My shoes don't fit anyone else. Not even me
sometimes.

Some people's shoes are fake. Some are real. Sometimes people's shoes are similar, however do not get confused. Cleanliness, comfort the weight that they can handle, envy, judgement, fake and real, shoes or no shoes – all these things determine the walks of life in which we come from.

THE WORLDS EXISTENTIAL CRISIS (SESTINA)

A –Born
B – Need
C- Stupidity
D- Accidents
E- Planned
F-Selfishness
Have we ever thought why we were born?
The answer could be from need.
Or it could simply be stupidity.
We are accidents.
We are planned, or we are both.
What we do know exists in all cases is
selfishness.

We ask why selfishness?
That only makes sense if we are accidents.
But it too connects with being planned.
In each case, it is the basis
for every human need.
The result is that we are all born.
We ask these questions already knowing yet
with a sense of stupidity.
Is wanting to know a sense of stupidity?
Wanting to know is justified selfishness.
Accidents happen, knowing is one of them.
The ultimate human question is knowing
why we were born.
It is the ultimate human need.
If God really dealt us His hand,
are we then all planned?
Wanting to know might give us different
answers than planned.
For we make assumptions – that there is the
real stupidity.
Yet wanting it is all justified not by want but
by need.

It feeds our worst enemy –selfishness.
All I know is that no one asked to be born.
And no one wanted to be an accident.
Lives can be turned upside down
by an accident.
Lives can be turned upside down if planned.
Remember, it's not their fault, they didn't ask
to be born.
Remember adults; think twice when stupidity
is masked by fun.
We are here because
sex is human selfishness.
We are here funnily enough because
sex is also a need.
So now I sit still, questioning this need.
Was I part of the accident?
Was I a product of human selfishness?
Was I planned?
Would it matter if I came from two
'responsible adults' and their stupidity?
I am in one big existential crisis of why
I was born.

ROBOTS OF THE WORLD

The day shines brightness
Their devices distract them
Robots of the world
Social media
Fakes people's intimacy
The world is a hoax
Are humans real now?
We are now digital slaves
Emotions are fake.

It seems nowadays society has become fake.
Fuck society.
The world is a big hoax thanks to social
media, faking intimacy and friendship

It's a challenge now for people to live with privacy, we are at rivalry.
How can it be acceptable to be unsocial yet social? You all know what I am talking about. Twitter, YouTube, video games, Facebook... these things are turning people into mindless robots. In a time of consumerism, how do we know what is real? Are celebrities? Heroes? I too am guilty of this, no one is not guilty. We love technology but to what extent? To the extent where we let it control our lives, let it control our spending with the invisible hand at play. To the extent of being socially awkward? Is this a generation of disorder or something greater because of technology? You tell me.

Kids and adults alike are living in their screens, too scared to come out of them. It is not an iPhone anymore. We all have iCocoons.

Can we find a class room now where students interact happily with one another at first encounters? Or a walking trail? No. Our eyes are glued to the screens. You know what's funny? I wrote this on my phone. Now isn't that ironic.

Version 2 Robots of the World (Free Verse Inspired by Mr Robot)

Fuck society, nowadays it's become fake
Friends with the eyes of snakes
No one cares about the heart ache
Listen up folks, for this is no joke
This world has become a hoax
Wouldn't piss on it to rid the fire,
I watch as it smokes
Social media faking intimacy and friendship
Mark Zuckerberg, 2016's ruler,
Lord let him end it
I hate the Zuckerberg dynasty
It is a challenge for people to live in privacy

Everyone is the paparazzi,
taking photos spitefully
Does God exist anymore? We need help we
are all at rivalry
Social yet antisocial, we are recluses
Using smart phones as our mind reduces
Twitter, YouTube, video games, Facebook
turning people into mindless robots
I wish these things the world would know not
How do we know what is real when
technology tells us how to feel?
Why does everyone worry about Facebook?
When there are children who can't even get
a meal
Now the only thing we care about is how
your face looks
Don't get me wrong technology is great but
to what extent?
To the extent where the invisible hand
spends your last cent?
Socially awkward, oh how society is tortured
We are a generation of disorder,

This is why I don't want a son or a daughter
Take a minute and look I wish you could,
But if you stood where I stood
you would see iPhones stealing childhoods
My face turns green
People living in their screens
All I want to do is scream
But everyone is selfish, no one can hear me
Everyone is part of a self-entitlement theory
I haven't seen a face look up from a phone in
a while it's eerie
Can we find places where people interact
happily at first encounters?
Don't answer that, the thought is literally
a downer
But we are all downers in a way
Looking down at phones every single day
If aliens could see the human race
They'd notice evolution went wrong, we are
a disgrace.

MOTHER EARTH

You are Killing Her!
(Free Verse Poem)

You are killing Her!
She gives you natural foods
You take all of it
She gives you animals
You kill them for trophies
She gives you water
You drain it dry
You are killing Her!
She gives you a breath of air
You blow poison gas in Her face
She gives you scenery
You tear up Her land for infrastructure
She gives you sunlight

You block it out with infrastructure
You are killing Her!
She gives you the stars
Your cities outshine them with forged light
She gives you snowy scenery
You melt it
You are killing Her!
She gives you the oceans
You dowse it with oil
She gives you fresh air
You make it artificial in your loungerooms
She gives you forests
You burn them down
You are killing Her!
She gives you clear skies
You fog them over
She brings YOU life
You bring Her death
You are killing Her!
She. Her. Mother Nature.
You, we as a species.
We. Are. Killing. Her. We have become robots
of the world.

We focus too much on technology and forget about the world.
The hand that feeds us, keeps us alive. The one thing Mother Nature does –
Is live for us. It's ironic isn't it…the one thing Mother Nature lives for is killing Her.
She gives us great beauties and now we only look at them through screens.
If we do not change as a species, as individuals – we are doomed.
People treat Earth like they have a right to her. Nobody owns the Earth.
The Earth is naïve.
As people have evolved as a species, the natural Earth has become naïve to our selfish tendencies,
Letting us take advantage of Her. Sometimes we hear her cry for help in the forms of natural disasters yet we kick her while she's down with global warming.
You, we are killing Her!

GAMING

Let's Play (Symbolism Poem)

"Portal" = "Playstation"

The portal takes me to worlds unknown
Allowing me to live multiple lives even if I die
It lets me interact with others
whenever alone
Adventuring everywhere challenges to defy
Shinning lights in dim rooms
Eventually I will need a break
The sound of each adventure booms
The portal makes my eyes ache
Transporting me away from reality

And away from worries and stress
The portal truly lets me become carefree
I can act how I like, no single one to impress
The portal giving me a life when I
have none outside
Come get lost with me and let's play, it's one
hell of a ride.

Go Hard or Go Home

We are home alone together at last. Propped against the pillows with the lights set to dim. I run my hands over your curvy, yet smooth body. You vibrate and lighten up to show me that you are turned on. I caress you with both hands, which eventually become sweaty. Tension and excitement is in the air as the anticipation of what is to come builds. I gently press your buttons making sure I touch each part of you. I wiggle my thumbs over your knobs until they become warm. The excitement is happening you vibrate to tell me when I am doing a good job, yet when

42

*I am doing something wrong you remain
still. I take a break, you lay on my chest,
warm and secure. The action comes back
to life as I pick you up ready to finish what I
started. The excitement builds and the finish
line is in sight, I grab you all flustered not
wanting to let you down. Satisfaction comes
over me, I can't hold it in anymore, I scream
a sigh of relief, the hard work paid off. I lay
on the pillows with you now in one hand
and the other over my eyes. I get up to get a
beverage after the game is over and the Xbox
controller is put away.*

GAMING THROUGH MY LIFE

GTA5 is on PS5 now... all hate aside it's actually a decent transfer to current gen and I for one still love this game. You can purchase it without breaking the bank which is the most important thing.

This does make me look back though. This game released in 2013 and I picked it up on ps3. My Mum took me to the midnight launch when they were still things. I played a lot of online with my cousin who I still keep in contact with to this day.

Fast forward to 2014/2015 when it was remastered and added first person mode. I picked it up on ps4 and Xbox one.

Fast forward to 2022. I'm still playing it. On ps5.

Where were you when it first released back in 2013, almost 10 years ago?
I was in high school – year 11, wanting to study IT and be a games developer. I would still love to get into IT again but nowadays I get too fidgety unless I'm 100% invested... even at my current job.

Where were you in 2014/2015 for the remaster? I was in Uni (started 2015), studying English & Creative writing, bored out of my brain, wasting my time and money and wondering if I was on the right path in life. If you can write, you can write, you don't need Uni for that.

Now – I work in a factory and am a home owner… and married!? Funny how you and your life change so much.

Moral of the story through the years = gaming has been a huge part of my life and in many ways, my escape from reality, my time to have fun and relax, hang with friends, etc. So many things change in life, but for me, I don't think gaming ever will.

HAIKUS

The Last Supper

They eat together
Jesus and his followers
Companions yet foes

Jesus forgives him
People betray all the time
Do reasons matter?

We too are the same
Help us forgive and forget
In the end, we die.

Headache

My head is throbbing
Studying with a headache
Brings nothing but tears.

FAMILY

– FAM(ILY)

Yup little brother, little bro
There's a place that I'd like to go
Back way before we started to grow
Before life started moving the opposite
to slow
Whoa
Step through my portal close your eyes and
picture this –
you, my buddy Luke and I playing Halo on
the couch
Parents came in like Oscar the grouch
Saying "The dog's gotten out!"
Flew up starting crying and frightfully
sooking

Until dad said "Let's go looking
Jaffa can't have gotten far
You three boys walk and I'll take the car"
Found ourselves on the oval nearby
searching for the family pet
Oh did I mention it was rainy and wet?
Anyway, we couldn't see a thing it was dark
And Jaffa wouldn't bark
so "Jaffa!" We decided to yell
Came across a ditch but was it holding
water? We couldn't tell
We volunteered Ryan to go first,
did he make it? "It's fine a bit of water but
not much" he tells
Friend and I step out and in we fell
We get out amongst the darkness and find
Dad with the dog
He finds three soaking boys tasked with
one job
Growing up together, he's my best bud
Got each other's back when life turns to mud

Never looking down on one another we hold
each other up
Always played as arbiter and chief,
Marcus and Dom
We're them now, not game characters but
that's where our brotherhood is from

Blood is always thicker in rough waters
Always, Yup
Our bond is strong our bond is big
I don't need to hide bodies, they help me dig
Blood is always thicker in rough waters
This ship isn't sinking

Big sister, only girl of us four
But growing up so much more
Used to call her my spare mum
just in case ours went flat
She taught me how to drive at night and
we'd chat
About nothing really, about this and that
Giving helpful life advice

Proof reading my school work
"Be more concise!"
She was the first I read my first poems to
Back then they were bad but she unjudgingly
let me do what I needed to do
I remember when she grew up
and out she moved
Almost every weekend I remember sleeping
over to the point where my bed was grooved
When she went to Kangaroo Island I cried
every day for a week straight
Before she left, she prepped a box of toys to
open each day she was gone, it was great
And something I'll always appreciate
For her return – It made it easy to wait
Ness, in times of stress
when life seems a mess
Your caring aurora helps guide me to success
Remember that time for year 8 art?
Got an assignment right at the term's start
Had to draw a portrait of myself but I knew
failure was in sight

You took the paper and drew all night
I passed
you said to take credit if anyone asked

Blood is always thicker in rough waters
Always, Yup
Our bond is strong our bond is big
I don't need to hide bodies, they help me dig
Blood is always thicker in rough waters
This ship isn't sinking

Big brother, the eldest of us all
Spent life looking up to you but not because
you're tall
You always kick some
Wise wisdom
You said never turn on fam
That hit me like oh damn
[That Stayed with me to this day]
Just like a lot of other things
When I think back
I see the joy my brother brings

Like when you came to my primary school for
sports day
I'd show you off and listen to what my friends
had to say
Or when I lost my balloon to that older kid
I started to cry, he saw you handed it back he
knew what he did
I think he ran off and hid
Or what about that time in your car you said
we could swear
I talked so much nonsense until I ran out
of air
I was having too much fun to care
From playing PS2 Vice City together
To staying overnight and watching walking
dead and falling asleep on couches
of leather
But wait
as I grow older I feel the more I can relate
I think we have a lot of the same taste
we're brothers I guess all that stuff is laced

16, you gave me my first wild Turkey,
refining my taste

When life starts to add pressure and squeeze
I don't have to wheeze and fall on my knees
Not when I have siblings like these

Blood is always thicker in rough waters
Always, Yup
Our bond is strong our bond is big
I don't need to hide bodies, they help me dig
Blood is always thicker in rough waters
This ship isn't sinking

When life starts to add pressure and squeeze
I don't have to wheeze and fall on my knees
Not when I have siblings like these
Now, now, now don't get me wrong,
I love lots more family members and could
go on and on
I just wrote this as I was feeling sentimental
towards my siblings I grew with

For my family, there isn't a thing I wouldn't
help you with
There isn't a thing I wouldn't do
Not just my siblings – my wife, parents,
aunts, uncles, cousins, nieces and nephew
There isn't a thing we can't get through
I love you all.

My Friends aka my 3 brothers

Luke – my oldest friend. Thank you for sticking with me ever since grade three. We have so many memories together. You are basically like family. All the sleep overs, Halo nights, talking about life, girls, jobs. All the laughs. You were the first person who's house I slept at during primary school. We grew up together and we shall grow old together.

Tyson – you were my first ever friend I made in high school. That wasn't the easiest place for me. I am forever grateful that we bonded over games in high school and that you got me into the uncharted series. As we grew older in Year 12, we bonded over movies and you are a huge reason as to why I have such a collection of movies. I'll never forget our tradition of leaving school early every Tuesday and getting Hungry Jacks. If you took a day off during school, I would rarely talk/ hang out with anyone until you returned. We shall grow old together.

Steven – you were my first friend I ever made through my working life. You made me realise that you were basically like me and that it was okay to be myself. Our mutual love for gaming will forever live in my mind. Playing Vita at work was a bonus! We host a podcast together and you were the idea behind me starting to be a streamer. I feel we are so alike; it is truly special. We shall grow old together.
You make going to work so much easier.

BROTHER (SONNET)

Don't you ever wonder?
Why we never see one another?
Why our relationship has gone under?
Why I simply can't talk to a brother
I still want things to change
Some things have, though not for the better
I imagine asking for a hug or two to
exchange
But it's been far too long, my eyes get wetter
I still carry your picture around in my pocket
I guess now in a way it's a symbol of hope
Speeding past your house – I'm the punk in
the rocket

I drive by to be closer to you
as a way to cope
My brother, for now we are parted
I just hope this relationship can be restarted.

DEPRESSION & ANXIETY

Raw Thoughts

I don't want to get into it but I hold a lot of
anger lately
About life – past, present, future,
it's increasing greatly
Listen here, sometimes I wish I could
disappear
Maybe that's why it's 4 a.m.
and I'm still awake
All by myself, no need to wear a mask
and be fake
See I'm not happy with who the fuck I am
But I hate change so these thoughts are a
fuckin scam
I am grateful for my life but I do not feel like
the man though

Lately I always feel I want to hide my face
like Mando
And to be honest, I fucking hate society
Some days I just want to ditch sobriety
Maybe I need therapy because running and
diving into games isn't working
The thoughts are still there lurking
But games are addicting though
Believe me I should know
Personality is incredibly addictive
Sometimes I can be ruthless, and savage,
and sadistic, and vindictive

"Do you believe people can change?
I don't think we can. Not really. I think we
come into this world who we are. And maybe
we get a little nicer. Or a little angrier. But we
can't change our fundamental nature."

These are the ugly thoughts my minds facing
My minds racing
I don't know if anyone really gets me not
even me

It's just sad to see
Got a pounding in my chest
I just want to be me,
fuck being the best

So hard on myself always applying pressure
Telling myself I'm the one who's lesser
There's so much overthinking
That now I'm just over thinking
Over it.

SOMETIMES YOU CAN BE YOURSELF

It's funny where life takes us
It can make and break us
I didn't want to write this but collectively
I feel like it's something I owe
Look I was at a point and it was kind of low
Overwhelmed with how much I didn't know
Scared as fuck to grow
Lots of dark thoughts
Thinking my life going to be short
Was feeling so lonely
Then I met the homies
Awkward at first but then it just clicked
Like all the boxes were ticked

I thought it was unlikely
But finally, I found people like me
I was a nervous wreck, anxiety flooding all
the way up to my neck
I just want to add – somehow, they helped
bring out a confidence within me I didn't
even know I had
Food for thought and I've got a plateful
And dudes, for that that I'm forever grateful
Always got the boys whenever motherfuckers
be making noise.

What is Sleep?

Another night I can't sleep
Tried counting sheep
But I've had enough of wool over my eyes
I am grateful for my life but I do not feel like
the man though
Always want to hide my face like Mando
And to be honest, I fucking hate society
Some days I just want to ditch sobriety
They are controlling us!
Freedom is an illusion
It's really a delusion
To rule, they use seclusion
they use fear
They use greed

The writing isn't on your wall it's on your
news-feed
Looking inside and my thinking is cooked it's
kind of fried
I just feel like every day I'm killing myself and
I'm not talking suicide
Come to think of it what would happen
if I died?
Who would miss me, I'm hoping someone
would've cried?
There's something I really need to fix
Because I don't care if I make it to 26
Again, not talking about suicide
I'm crystal clear
So, listen with your middle ear listen here
I just feel like I want to sometimes
disappear.

I Just Want

Everyday Life
I just want to chill
I just want to chill
No more stress, a little more chill
Living dollar bill to bill
Work is lining me up and it's looking to kill
But I know the drill
This is just part of the deal
Do this not for the thrill
maybe one day use my niche skill
But until then I just want to chill
No more stress, a little more chill
You're probably thinking
"C'mon Jordan be real"

Yeah, fuck it
I got the world on my shoulders
In other words, I hold my own
Isis on these minds, they are blown
You don't have bars, but you should because
what you're doing is criminal
Playing this shit so minimal
I have the good shit, it's so drinkable
It's unthinkable to think y'all so cynical
I would swear to God but I can't get any more
biblical

Sorry, I just want to chill
Just want to chill
No more stress, a little more chill
Gimme more games
Because from where I'm stood at
They're the only thing I'm good at
I just want to chill
I use to really want to be the man
Now I just want to do what I can
I just want to chill
Stressed

Depressed
Who would've guessed?
Got a pounding in my chest
I just want to be me, fuck being the best
I just want to chill
Just some life shit I can't stop thinking about.
Had to write this
I tried and realised I can't fight this
So, let's begin...
I am no expert on integrity and I'm not of pure pedigree
I know I'm not perfect but I'm happy with me
End of the day, the one who lives with me is me
All the anxiety and bullshit when happiness felt so deprived
I'm glad I strived
I'm glad I survived
I'm proud Looking back from where I started to where I arrived
The ride isn't over,
confidence slowly being revived

75

I'm an adult now I'm grown,
challenging my comfort zone
And still will never know about what I
should've known
But I fuckin hold my own
I'm updating myself,
always working on my coding
Sometimes I wonder why to myself
I was so mean

Addictive personality, games music movies
alcohol and codeine
I thought it was helping me with coping
But now it's movies and games
It's still an addiction ingrained in my brains
But it could be worse so fuck your judgement
You can judge, I won't hold a grudge
That shit gets heavy and for that
I'm just not ready
Just pop something on the telly and I
become the main character for the night
Hero, villain, gangster, millionaire, movies

make me who I am and fight for me when
I can't fight
I jump in and my TV becomes a portal
Adventures and interesting lives,
I feel immortal
I know I'm not perfect but I'm happy with me
Yeah, happy with me
I don't even know if I want to share this,
it's tender
And I'm glad I've met some new
family members
Shits crazy, I don't have a PHD in psych
But I can tell we are very much alike
I'm so happy, never get me wrong
Never get me wrong
These family members, in my life is where
they belong
It just makes me think, the kids just miss out
on so much when adults fight
And shit happens I know but you can't say
I'm not right
And right here, and right now

To never let it happen again is what I vow
I'm just grateful that shits passed
Only good feelings on blast
Here's to making memories that last
I know I'm not perfect
but I'm happy with me.

Tired

Straight up, I just wanted to get this off my chest
Feeling stressed, angry, lost, a bit depressed
Just want to apologise if I've been different toward you
There's some I'd tell to fuck off, suck a dick if I could afford to
Wouldn't hesitate
See those who mean the most to me – for you I'd give my all
Until I fuckin fall
And even still I'd fuckin crawl
See all I do is game and write
That and with my brain I fight

All these choices, all these voices sometimes
all they do is shout
All I really want to do is block them out
Stranger danger, right? So why am I talking
to myself? I don't know who I am
I know I want to be good
My biggest fear is letting you down
That feeling is enough to make you drown
Now don't get it twisted, I'm not talking
about suicide – Sometimes I just don't want
to be here – I don't want to die
Just too tired to cry too tired to try, just want
to hide No more energy always fuckin tired
no longer inspired
These days the one I see around my house
most is the man delivering the post
Every fuckin day is a fight
No, I am not alright
Got no vision, losing my sight
My world feels dim, not so bright
Every day is a fight
Help
Every day is a fight

A fight inside my head
A fight to get out of bed
A fight to put up with crap
A fight to not snap
A fight to not rage
A fight to not feel trapped
A fight to go to sleep
A fight to stay awake
A fight to say a peep
I'm always trying to be a better man
Have a better plan
Feels like I never can
Take me back to simplicity, neverland
All the voices inside my head are liars and
they're dumb
I wanted to post this but this thinking might
scare some
And I hate changes
I can't talk to strangers
I'm stuck in my comfort zone
But I'm toxic, better off alone
Truthfully, I wish I could do something
usefully

But usually
I never do
And I cringe at the person I use to be
Cringe
Yup hanging by a hinge
Sorry I don't mean to winge, I feel I taint
everything in a negative tinge.

THINKING TO MYSELF

Sometimes I wonder why to myself
I am so mean
Addictive personality, games music movies
alcohol and codeine
Really just anything that lets me escape
Or just anything that stops me from feeling
like being me
They're like BnE
telling me 'I'll be there for you'
'Even when you are blue'
Maybe it's fuckin true
But at what cost?
Maybe I should admit, I'm fucking lost

And this year feels so fucking hard even
though I've been trying and trying
Fuckhead invaded our space, houses fallen
through, just lost my job
and even my dog dying
Spent most of this bullshit year crying
Prayer position I'm down on my knees
Life got a gun to my head,
trigger ready to squeeze
I can't be bothered asking please
Heart feeling like Darth Vader
Happiness feeling like fader

That's probably why I'm addicted
to TV and movies
Because whenever I'm feeling gloomy
Just pop on something on the telly and I
become the main character for the night
Hero, villain, gangster, millionaire, movies
make me who I am and fight for me when I
can't fight

I jump in and my TV becomes a portal
Adventures and interesting lives,
I feel immortal
Then comes the end of the movie
Again, I'm feeling gloomy
Face back to droopy
So now I go back to finding my next flick
Fuck how my brain ticks.

This Game of Life

I just don't get it, maybe forget it
Actually nah, if I keep silent, I will regret it
People say life isn't a game and that's a
damn shame
If only they could all think the same
Then they would see what I'm trying to claim
What the fuck am I on about
Yeah, life is a game, just hear me out
You see, we're all trying to level up
Breaking our backs, working like the
devil yup
Trying to progress to that very next stage
in our life
Before we reach that next age in our life

have that next wage or cause a strife
We are either succeeding or fighting
The graphics are so real, must be
that lighting
We either got demon souls or halos
Levels man, get high or lay low
Mashing, mashing, my brain is sore
This thinking isn't uncharted, we can be
gods of war
I'm hanging with a league of legends and
when we begin day 1 of life – bloodborne
Why do so many people want to even
the score?
All I see is everyone killing themselves
jumping for that next coin
Dude, we got no checkpoints
Get consoled all of a sudden
We're all controlling and pushing buttons
Life is like a game, either losing or slaying
And we're all playing
Some disconnect or are staying
It's just strategy, you might not realise

Just take a look with real eyes
mini-games like dancing, driving, running,
and sex
(Oh, so that's why I press triple ex)
the key to winning is
managing your resources
Just got to run whatever the course is
Life is a video game, all wired weird inside
They're all watching live you can't hide
We're all made up of different coding
That explains why I haven't had my coffee
and having trouble loading
I had a dream that I died
And I gave them this poem
as a strategy guide
I just don't get it,
maybe forget it.

HELLO FRIEND

You wake up in the later stages of morning, if it can be still classified as morning. You don't mean to.
It makes you grumpy towards those around you... not good. You are sorry about that and don't mean it. Be grumpy at yourself not them.
Your eyes are tired and heavy just like your brain. They stay that way all day. No matter what you do, no matter how much coffee you drink, no matter how much you try to rest. The thoughts come back and fuck your brain until it hurts and gives you a headache. But the noise, the noise distracts you.

You don't realise it's your thoughts doing this to you. You nurse the headache like a weeping infant until night falls upon you. For some reason the stresses of the waking day are too much. Too much noise. The moon transforms a lethargic you into an energetic and awake you, like a werewolf. It's night now. You see your partner and spend time with them. You play online games with your brother and friends until it gets late. They go offline. You are alone again. Dark. Quiet. Freedom?... but also, depressing? How? The quiet is soothing, this is time for you... but the thoughts come back again. You can't tell if it is enjoyable or shit, maybe you've gotten used to it?

Or do you depend on it, like it keeps you grounded? Unsure. You need to sleep. The next day is calling your name like a drill Sargent in the distance. Demanding your full attention to do stupid shit to make stupid people happy. Okay. You

lay in bed. You can't sleep even though you should be fucking exhausted.
It's like you want to stay awake as long as possible just to hold onto what's left of the day, what's left of your time... because you know times will eventually change.
They always do, you know that.

Hello old friend. There you are, you have come to visit me again and talk. You bring up the past a lot, and insecurities which is stupid but I let you ramble. Maybe it's healthy to listen to you let it out. You, the thoughts, force yourself upon me like a cigarette stained, drunkard sleaze hitting on a girl in the back of a bar... 11 p.m. turns into 11 p.m., 1 a.m. turns into 4 a.m., and so forth. You can no longer lay down. It makes it easier for the thoughts to penetrate you. What about all of those things you said to your partner? Did you treat her like shit? How about your friends? You're not a good friend.

And your family? What about your life, huh?
You won't make anything of it.
You could but you doubt it.
You hope you have a good future and don't
fuck anything up... you start thinking about
the good aspects of how you want to shape
your future... as if for a few minutes there
is clarity. But it fades. Sometimes you tell
others these desires for your future but you
never act on them so it looks like you talk
a bunch of shit... but only you know it's the
truth. You feel stupid but right but wrong
but sad... you're... shit you used the wrong
"your" it must be late. YOUR old friend is
bringing up a lot. You start to sink into your
mattress. Your blankets weigh tons as they
sit on your chest, you gasp for air, wrestle the
blankets and throw yourself up, out of that
sinking hole? No, sinking mattress. Got to
keep busy. You watch a movie, play a game,
write, read. But never create. No, that part
of you is dying. You're just a hollow shell of
what you could be.

You are a shadow, the light and creative energy drips out when you cry mainly. But you haven't cried in a while. You just can't be bothered with it. Sometimes the creativity comes back but it mostly just teases you. Cunt. You put some lo-fi hip hop mixes on and eventually, the soft piano keys and drum loops lull your mind. It helps you think of relaxing dreams. You eventually fall asleep... one tiny phone illuminating itself in the dark helps ease and calm you. It's quite the site. It lights up your room in the right ways. Not too bright, just a gentle light... a gentle light amongst these thick dark patches of uncertainty. As you fall asleep, your muscles twitch in rhythm to the piano keys and drum loops. You fall asleep thinking fuck the world but don't fuck the world at the same damn time. You wake up in the later stages of morning, if it can be still classified as morning. You don't mean to.

STAIN

Panicking and overthinking, I think my mind
is fried
I'm a burden to so many, maybe I should
have died
Late nights in tears, I can't count the amount
I have cried
Disappointing so many friends, I know it
looks the opposite but I have tried

A lot of my relationships have an
anxiety stain
All because I cannot get out of my brain

*Make plans, pull out last minute, letting
people down, causing pain
Listen they say "It's nothing new,
Jordan's at it again"*

*I'm sorry, no I'm not, fuck you,
sympathise for me
Now I'm all alone, burnt bridges and people
to the third degree
I'm shaking, pleading with myself and my
girlfriend I'm on my knees
I hope things get better in this supposed
future I cannot see*

*They say it's an uphill battle, but this is a
mountain and I'm falling
Isolating myself further, no longer answer
the phone when it's calling
I can't seem to move forward, I keep stalling
Maybe it's the weight of this sadness that
I'm hauling*

All my friends and family know is my
depressed and anxious side
Whenever we talk there's a clear strain

I want it to end so I plea and plea
I want my thoughts to stop brawling.

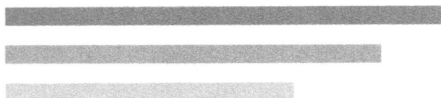

TALKING TO MYSELF

I think I'm alright
(No, you're not)
I think I can trust my thoughts
(They lie to you)
I don't need to overthink anymore
(Don't be stupid, you need to with
everything)
My mind is clean and quiet
(Your mind is a mess, it's LOUD and a riot)
I need to trust myself and others
no more paranoia
(Never! They all hate you, you're the one
who's in the wrong)
I feel strong sometimes

(But you're still so weak)
I want to close my eyes and drift off
(Lie with your eyes open
starring at the ceiling)
Just breathe
(Panic! Motherfucker!)
I'm really sorry
(No, you're not, do you even care)

Get out, do something, be productive!
(You'll lay in bed all day, and you'll cry)
I want to be alive
(Kill yourself, stop being a burden)
I didn't want to let you down
(Yes, you did, you made plans
knowing you would)
Stop... please
(Hahahaha)
I think my friends and family like me
(They have a better time with others
than with you)
Hopefully one day I'll be successful

(You are and always will be a fuck up)
I want things to go smoothly
(You WILL ruin everything)
I'm calm and love those around me
(SNAP AT EVERY-FUCKING-THING THEY SAY)
I understand some may not understand me
and that's okay
(They hate you and will never understand so
fuck them)
I want to stop and think of others, maybe
help them
(FUCK them, YOU have me to focus on)

I think I might be learning
(You're lying to yourself)
I can do it; I know I can
(You can do it? Why haven't you already?)
My mind is strong
(You need to rely on medications)
I'm will not be selfish
(You already are)
I will get better

(You're fucked)
Maybe I'm childish...
(Finally, we can agree on something, keep going)
FUCK YOU!
(FUCK YOU!)

Maybe God Was Listening

Been a few months now
I still think of suicide
I'm ashamed of it

I still sit inside
Still isolating myself
I let them all down

I'm scared of my brain
I have told my girlfriend now
She's a little scared

Girlfriend is helping
Appreciate her so much
Intake at headspace

Learning ways to cope
Challenging my thoughts and brain
Headspace, months away

I'm still scared and sad
Girlfriend is so supportive
Want to marry her

I don't feel alone
So much support from my girl
One knee, she said yes

My friends don't hate me
That's what my fiancé said
Thoughts are steadying

We are married now
I have a person for life
Headspace will start soon

Headspace went so well
I think it could really help
Thank you to my wife.

Hi

Let me introduce myself
Just thought I'd let you know
Old Jordan is thrown on the shelf
Therefore, this is Jordan 2.0

I've been praying, I've been praying
so damn long
In fact, I'm still in shocked it happened
I am no longer weak I am strong
Building myself up from what I flattened

For so long I was stuck inside my mind
I was lost and had no map

My eyes sewed shut, completely blind
Tore my eye-lids off now I see this crap

Now I can see and fight and take aim
Challenging these thoughts
I no longer feel fear or fake or shame
I feel great, but hold the applause

Sometimes the beast will come back
and try to bite me
But now I don't pay it much care or time
I now know how to fight me
I feel great, finally in my prime

So much has changed in a year
Building, married man, working man
Life has never been so clear
I feel great, goddamn!

Many thanks to my wife who was sent to me
You supported me in times that were really
tough

You and me, we are meant to be
And Chewie distracting me every time he
says "Ruff"

No more questioning, over thinking,
stressing or thoughts of death
No more late nights lying awake
I can finally catch my breath
Starting headspace because I finally know
what's at stake

I am Jordan 2.0, 2.0
There had to be pain in order to grow
I re-programmed myself, woah
Just thought I'd let you know

Anxiety, I'll always be what you're stuck to
But I just wanted you to know:
Fuck you!

MISSING OUT

Anxiety has caused me to miss out on my friends. I have drifted away with some if not all. I've missed some of their big moments like 18th's, 21st's, house warmings, or just general hanging out. To my friends (you know who you are) I deeply apologise. It feels like nothing is getting better and I'm sinking into a dark hole that spirals down into nothing but loneliness. I understand the damage I've done to you all. Fuck anxiety. I'm sorry.

INNER DEMONS

God, hit me up, answer the phone,
I'm calling your line
I know you hear this because
I'm calling all the time
Pick up I need to talk I need a chat
Right now, I'm feeling flat
I don't know where my head is at
I'm scared and angry at myself
Because of the decline of my mental health
I just really need to know what to do
Please just answer, I really need you
I've had enough, just had enough
I'm not just bitching; I say this with
conviction

Just had enough
I am weak and not so tough
Every day feels pretty rough
I've had enough of feeling like a failure even
though I'm really trying
I've had enough of spending most of my days
and nights crying

I've had enough of everyday
being some sort of fight
I've had enough of having no vision, no sight
I've had enough of pushing my friends away
I've had enough of waking up every day
Just had enough
So much happening in my mind
I don't mean to scare you with what you find
I just want to say sorry to my wife
She doesn't need a shitty husband like me
in her life
And I've been addicted, I can't lie
It's calling again but I let is pass by
Why?

I don't want to fail my wife
I will fight and the right decisions
I will try to choose
Because her, I never want to lose
I don't want to fail my wife
But I'm in so much pain from life
Every beat my heart feels pierced
with a knife
Please don't judge, just be fuckin kind
I just want a lighter mind
So hard on myself
Why am I so hard on myself?

Always telling myself I am lesser
Natural born fuckin stressor
Most fucked up out of Vernon, Ryan, Vanessa
So, God hit me up where you at?
I really need a fucking chat.

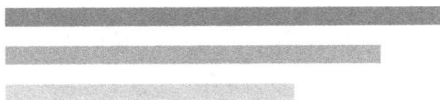

FIGHT

Every day is a fight
No, I am not alright
Got no vision, losing my sight
My world feels dim, not so bright
Every day is a fight
Help

Every day is a fight
A fight inside my head
A fight to get out of bed
A fight to put up with crap
A fight to not snap
A fight to not rage
A fight to not feel trapped in a cage

A fight to go to sleep
A fight to say a peep

I know I'm not easy to live with
Nope nope nope
Feel like I could snap like Ani in
"Revenge Of The Sith"
I've lost a new hope
Every morning I wake up like
Why am I here? The anxiety strikes
People, I'm no good
I can't stand myself; I don't think you should
Can't talk to people, wish I could
Annoy them, can I stop, wish I would
But no matter what I do I somehow
fuck up things
And sadness is the only thing my heart brings
Wish I could fly from this life,
grow some wings
Sometimes I dream of a life of bliss
Everyday my mind goes something like this
People don't love being around me

I'm selfish
I'm rude to lots of people
Can't make decisions
I need to be better

They didn't even rhyme, oh well
Maybe because this is a cry for help, oh hell

Every day is a fight
No, I am not alright
Got no vision, losing my sight
My world feels dim, not so bright
Every day is a fight
Help

Losing myself to this world
What I do know is
I need prayers, big man upstairs could use
some help of his
I feel no matter how hard I try
I get in the way
I'm awkward and don't say what
I want to say

Unless it's a poem for the website
But fuck the site
Fuck the site
No one reads it anyway I know I'm right
But yet here I am, still I write
I hate my brain
FUCK this constant pain

I'm so over thinking
Because now I'm overthinking
Thoughts of hopelessness and that I'm
forever sinking
Try to sleep but feel crushing pressure
on my chest
So now I'm just tired and stressed

Every day is a fight
No, I am not alright
Got no vision, losing my sight
My world feels dim, not so bright
Every day is a fight
Help

It's sad that these days the one I see at my house the most
Is the man delivering the post?
These days the postie is the only one to make the doorbell chime
I haven't seen my friends for a long time
I know my wife has had a hard time
Being connected to me is an uphill climb
I don't blame you; you can stay away it's my fault I'm too hard
I'm always on my guard

It's hard
I want to be normal just give me a slither or shard
I can't tell if I'm angry at my friends, wait
I'm angry at me!
Why can't they see!?
No, it's not them it's me.

Every day is a fight
No, I am not alright

115

Got no vision, losing my sight
My world feels dim, not so bright
Every day is a fight
Help

I struggle to make decisions
There is a constant division
I might look fine to your vision
But inside
I feel so disconnected from reality
I'm just an absentee
I don't mean it
Quiet on the outside but look within
Clawing to get out of my skin

Banging my head against a wall
Crying so much I could fill a pool
Screams, constant screaming
Constantly bad dreaming
Voices yelling
What are they telling?
"Don't be so awkward"

How?
"Don't be so quiet"
How?
"You're being lazy"
Am I? I-
"YOU'RE WORTHLESS"
"WASTE OF SPACE"
"YOU'LL NEVER BE GOOD ENOUGH"
"SO NAIVE"
"YOU'RE A PIG"
"YOU'RE NOTHING"
"YOU GET IN THE WAY"
"YOURE AN IDIOT"
"YOU KNOW NOTHING"
"YOURE NOT DOING IT RIGHT"
'YET ANOTHER SCREW UP"
Shut the fuck up
Leave me alone
So, if you see me, lights on
but no-one home

Or if I can't make decisions, or seem dumb
or sad or am snappy, I don't mean it, I'm just
preoccupied and numb
Everything I say or do is a fight
But I don't want to fight
I just want to do right
Something isn't right
I'm just so tired, trying to fight myself
so tired
Therapist, you're hired

Every day is a fight
No, I am not alright
Got no vision, losing my sight
My world feels dim, not so bright
Every day is a fight
Help

If I seem like I'm having trouble there's just
too much noise
Too much chatter
That's what's the matter

Oh, hi anxiety, what's up depression?
Oh, you want to chat,
time for another session?
Okay
Well
I'm putting my all into you till I'm drained
Trying to fix my head, leaving it pained
Even when I'm good you're still there,
my mind is stained
Shaking sitting peacefully but
I just want to scream and now
I have a pain in my gut
FUCK YOU
Yeah, fuck you
Yes, I said fuck you
You're the one that takes my energy
And with the insults oh so generously
You put me in a bad mood
You make me the token shy and awkward
dude
Giving me headaches
Putting pressure on me till I snap and my
head breaks

Kidnapped me from my family and friends
Making me make sure my life ends
So yeah, fuck you
Fuck you
I said fuck you
Don't ever try to disturb me again

I feel it when
You try to get under my skin
I'll always fight you, forcing my grin
I've really got no more choices
I really have to block these voices
Really have to get myself better
Only feel safe at home, in my sweater
Doctor hurry up and write me a letter
Just make me better

Every day is a fight
No, I am not alright
Got no vision, losing my sight
My world feels dim, not so bright
Every day is a fight
Help

You're probably reading this and thinking
Jordan has seemed good whenever I've
asked it
Chances are I've probably masked it
Feels like it'll be that way till I'm in a casket
So please
I understand if you want to just
Leave me alone
I'm better that way

No one to disappoint there's nothing to say
Chances are no-one will read this
I don't even know what my point is
I'm sorry
Oh, wait now I see
No one to blame but me.

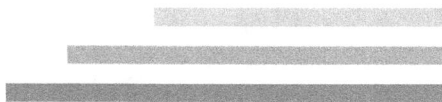

THE ANXIETY MONSTER

This anxiety is a beast
And on my soul, it will feast
So that's what's the matter
I can feel the monster lining my soul
up on a platter
But I will stand and fight, big or small
I will get up after the fall
I briefly met Jordan 2.0
And then he had to go
But I can do it again I know we will meet
For I realise now I am never beat
If there's anything I've learned
Is anxiety might leave bridges burned

And it wants you to forget
Yeah, it wants you to forget
It wants you to forget every single time
you've won the battle and
been filled with pride
It wants you to remember every time it's
broken your stride
It wants you to forget that you can hide
But the truth is, you can fight inside
The monster inside, fuck it up good
For those thinking "Oh I wish I could"
You really can if we unite
Let's go hunting monsters in our dark night
These monsters are powerless without us
These monsters should be the ones kicking
up a fuss
This monster will always be a part of me
And there will be a constant fight for my
brain cell key
But it's a fight I can't do alone
I need loved ones in my zone
So anytime your monster wants you to
believe you blew it

123

Just remember you've already gotten
through it
Stand hand in hand,
tonight we go monster hunting,
let's do it.

HOW MY MIND THINKS

How does my mind think?
How does my mind think?
Sometimes it makes me think
Sometimes it makes me believe
instead of swimming I will sink
Sometimes it is just edging on the brink
Sometimes it's knotted and confused,
got a couple of kinks
It gets overwhelmed with how fast things
move, it's all over before you blink
Sometimes it makes me happy and feel good
Like if I had to take on the world, I could
It makes me realise how much I have grown
And I've finally become a man of my own

Feel like I got life figured out
then realise how much I don't know
Most the time though
It's got me feeling low
Happiest when I rhyme
When I play with words all the time
Or when I ride my bike
When I watch a movie or play a game
Other than that, I'm worrying
and that's a damn shame
It feels like I'm a natural born stressor

So hard on myself always applying pressure
Telling myself I am lesser
There's so much overthinking
That now I'm just over thinking
Over it
Letting friends down;
curse this anxious brain
Lotta my memories have an anxiety stain
But I have to remember I can be strong like
Bane

*Sometimes I hate my thinking and the way
I'm wired
It just makes me tired
But then again if I wasn't me then I couldn't
play with words like no one else can
I love creating it makes me feel like the man
Goddamn
I'm a writer and that means I'm a fighter
Don't understand?
Look at the Samurai and their haikus
Now you understand why it's poetry I choose
Look, I know we have good and bad days
I'm just saying my brain thinks in all these
different ways
Despite the bad, I still work at my passion
every day
No matter how much doubt
I'll never take the easy way out.*

LOVE

Year One

1 year – not that long ago
I still relive it in my head though

1 year since our wedding

Our special day

down the aisle you walked and a tear
I was shedding

2 little but significant words we had to say

"I do"
Because I love you

Through thick and thin, riches and wealth
Happy, sad, sickness and health
"I do"
Because I love you

Through hard times and of joy
Through it all, with you, I will endure and
enjoy

My dear wife,
I cannot think about what I would do
without you
in my life

I know it has been a hard year,
Full of tears, joy and fear
But most of all, we have stuck together
Never leaving one another's side
No matter how much we want to
run and hide
You have and always will be my rock,
my light,
my strength

*Helping me though depression and anxiety
and my fears.
You have been and always will be
my beautiful wife.*

*You make me proud in everything you do
I hope I make you proud as much as you
make me proud.*

*You are the most perfect wife; you deserve
the world. Words do not do you justice.
We have accomplished so much together
already.
I cannot wait to buy a house with you.
We are each other's shoulder to cry on,
to lean on, protect each other,
build each other up
and unconditionally love each other...
I think this year has proved this fact
I am yours, forever loyal and grateful.*

*I am so grateful for you. To have you. To be
with you. I love you so much.
Thank you for being an amazing person,*

never change who you are.
Thank you for being my wonder wife.

I love that I can talk to you, that you never judge, that we like each other's company and watching TV together. At the end of a hard day, laying with you and watching TV is so soothing and calming.

Here is to many, many, many more years together as a married couple. Our life is just beginning. Happy Anniversary, my beautiful wife. I love you so much.
Erica,
I vow to stand by your side and to love and support you unconditionally for better or worse, rich or poor, in sickness and health. You are such a kind and loving, selfless soul – through this, you have taught me what it is to love selflessly. I give my all to you. Every time you feel alone, scared, helpless or sick – I want you to look down at your wedding ring and remember it as a symbol that you have me no matter what. Just like

your ring, my commitment, love, respect and patience to you is never-ending and strong. I will do my utmost in life to give you the best I can and love you to the fullest. I am yours. Forever. Our souls intertwined. A team. Our whole time together thus far, you've pushed me towards becoming the best I can be. I vow to push you to be the best you can be (which is pretty hard now because you're pretty much perfect). When you feel weak, when you fall, when you give up on yourself – look by your side and I will not be standing there... no, I will be down with you, picking you up, helping you, no judgement. I will lift you up and lean you on me, carrying both our weight. Will it be heavy or a burden? No. Why? Because our love is strong and unconditional. Erica, I vow to love you until the day I die. And even then, we will meet in the next life. I love you, my dear wife.

MISSING YOUR SMILE

I've been meaning to write this
for a while now
It's been a minute since I see you smile now
I just want you to know
what you mean to me
How important you are,
you make me feel free
I'm so thankful I bent that knee
But you see my heart is fuckin sore
Just wish I could give you more
I know I don't give you much and I should
I know you say it's good

*But it's incredibly selfish from where
I'm stood
Not making excuses but I think I get too
wrapped up in my heroes
They help when I feel not so super,
slowing to zero
I would say you mean the world to me
but that's a lie
Because sometimes this world is shit
and I'd rather die
No, you're my galaxy, my universe
More than the world, there when it hurts
For better or worse
I'm so proud of you
For everything you've done
and what you will do
I'm always on your side
Staring with pride
We're in this ride
together, Bonnie and Clyde
When your eyes are wet or dried
I want to be there to guide*

Please don't hide
Me and you forever, you are the best
Fuck the rest
Whenever there's a problem and you feel
rock bottom
Just remember you got your Gollum
You're so precious to me
and I can't ever lose you
I will always choose to
love you even when you refuse to
I will always choose you
don't let it confuse you
You're the one I am glued to
So many good qualities I look at you in awe
I want to be like you, I can't help but adore
Your tender touch I love it so much
Never lose who you are
I know you've got 1 scar 2 scar
Keep glowing bright like a star
I can't wait for you to be the mother of my
child now

I've been meaning to write this
for a while now
It's been a minute since I saw you smile now

- I love you ♥ .

HEADLIGHTS & PIANO BEATS

Headlights and piano beats
Through these streets
That's thinking time
Hope I don't get a speeding fine

Night-time is the right time
Headlights and piano beats
Through these streets
That's thinking time
I could be at home drinking wine
I could be in the city going out
of my freaking mind
But no no no

No no no
That's my thinking time
You're on my mind
Like Bino on his grind
You're a queen in this game of chess
But
I can see you're stressed, I see you're stressed
Killing yourself to live, working up the sweats
You have two planets on your chest
I'm not talking about your breasts
The weight of the world, let alone mine – just
know I got the rest
Juggling the weight of two worlds, I didn't
mean to do this to you I'm perplexed
Yes
We can do this, it's not over yet
Let's
get away and chill, get rid of everything
complex
Diamond in the rough
Keep it cool and handle your stuff

Headlights and piano beats
Through these streets
That's thinking time
Hope I don't get a speeding fine

Your vision is dimming because you can't see
your mission
living life in this colour is sort of funny
Life's journey has more curves than a
Playboy bunny
And I don't have much money,
I'm sorry though, you will get your honey
You are mine, call me Whinnie
Together, we are winning
You've got some insecurities
(Who doesn't)
I know you don't think you're enough
But your mind lavishes in purity
You are strong, you are tough
Your eyes rain
Let me take away your pain
So many naysayers, fuck them bitches –
hew Hefner

Because, together we are the better,
they are the lesser
No matter of the weather, we rise
and they will never
I may not yet be ready
Nervous belly nervous nelly
But you stick by me, heady. You stick by me
keeping steady, haven't left me

Headlights and piano beats
Through these streets
That's thinking time
Hope I don't get a speeding fine

Yeah, these waters are uncharted yet you are
my artifact
Bet you're smiling now, that's the art-of-fact
Doing so much without questions and
putting yourself second
Putting up in my anxious times
We'll be together in our ancient times
I'm smiling as these lights hit my face

Driving in this crazy damn rat-race
I'm chilling, window down, in my feelings
For you I could improve, got some things I
need to prove
I got some bad habits but they're monsters
waiting to be killed, so have at it, stab at it
Happy memories keep on stacking
Happy memories keep on stacking
It's like this was meant to happen
Got that smile, laugh, that hair nobody else
could match
So if you fall, if you fall, just know
you are a catch

Kids, if they can put up with you
acting stupid
You know you've been hit by cupid
Headlights and piano beats
Through these streets
That's thinking time.

POCKET POEM

DREAM

For my Nephew and Nieces – I love you all!
Never stop following your dreams
Because life is never as hard as it seems
Whenever you have fear
Those who love you will be here
You can do so much right
Whenever you need me, I'll be in sight
Everything will be alright
You've got lots of courage,
you don't need to find it
And whatever you do in life,
I'll be behind it.

Losing a Pet

CHEWIE

My heart hurts for you
Everything we've been through
There for me when I was blue
Our bond was true

I'll never forget our time together
You'll be in my heart forever
I miss you always
You would protect me all ways

Our walks, cuddles, play or sleeps
So many cherished moments, my heart
weeps
I hope you're in heaven and again we meet

You'll always be my good boy
and that's a feat
Never leave me, watch down on me and
I'll never fail
When I reach those clouds, I hope to see
your wagging tail

You trusted me to look after you
I trusted you to look after me
My first ever buddy to help with my demons
You're so important words cannot explain

And I'm sorry you went to sleep but you were
causing too much pain
Aggressiveness but ended humane
Our love will always remain
Me and you will always be a pack
And that's a fact I got your back
I love you, Chewie.

DREAMING & CREATIVITY

Never Stop Sleeping In

Your life dreams can be a powerful force.
They can overwhelm us, fill us with
regret. They can inspire us and give us
determination.
They can be tiresome. They can be worth it.
They can be realistic... or not.
Dreams can be time consuming.
They say that dreams only come
when you sleep.
A word of advice for your dreams:
Never give up.
Never stop dreaming.

If your boss asks why you were late to work,
tell them you were following your dreams...
it sounds better than sleeping in.
Never stop sleeping in.

CREATIVITY HAS 4 LEGS

Creativity is like a dog.
It never comes to call. Rather, when it wants
to come to you it will.
When it does come to you for scratches, it is
often at the most inconvenient timing.
You might be sleeping, washing up, driving,
in the shower.
If you are busy, it does not stop barking
in your ear.
You cannot force a dog to sleep,
same with creativity.
It needs that scratch to be itched and will not
rest until you do it.
Only stopping when you rush to write

*whatever idea you have so it doesn't
fade away.
If you lose your creativity, you feel heartbroken,
sad, like a piece of yourself is missing.
When lost, you realise you took all the
barking and inconvenient timing for granted.
When found, you are over the moon! Holding
it tightly and feeling the joy radiating from it.
Sometimes when two people with
creativities meet. They play off one another.
Tails wagging.
Your creativity always wants to be fed.
Even if it just ate. It is relentless.
Sometimes it can reflect the type of life lived.
Peaceful, hostile, happy, depressed.
If your creativity bites people, opens their
eyes, that might be a sign.
Most of all, creativity needs you
and you need it.
Keep walking it, training it, feeding it.
Never stop interacting with it.*

BOY

BOY

Creativity is like a dog.
Hello, Boy. I will not use your real name in
this for the sake of privacy.
You were my first pairing when I became an
SSO.
I wasn't sure how to interact with you at first.
You were very quiet. A kid in the system.
You needed someone consistent.
You needed someone calm.
Boy, I saw a lot of myself in you.
You wore your sweatshirt constantly, hoodie
up, hiding your face.
If only you knew how many times I,

*as an adult, would pull my hoodie up
whenever I wanted to shut out the world.
You were anxious, fiddling with your fingers.
I could relate. I was anxious most days I
clocked in for work at that school.
I could feel your anxiety and for some
strange, unexplainable reason,
it stopped mine.
It was like I was focused on trying to help
you, because I knew what monster you were
dealing with.
Some days were good for you, some bad.
Good days, we would talk about video
games. You loved Fortnite. I played it too. We
would talk about our games.
This is how I would reach you, distract you
from trying to hide.
Hoodie up, head on desk, hiding. Until I
asked if you wanted to go to the library,
somewhere less noisy. Somewhere where
you felt less of an outsider. It was here we
would talk about games.
For that moment in the libraries, you forgot.*

About the bad.
Don't get me wrong, I could relate to you,
but you also had demons I could never
understand.
Sometimes you would have outbursts.
Swear, throw things about. Whatever else.
Whilst I didn't like you doing this, I
understood why.
You couldn't stand the thought of failing.
Honestly, I understand that. Same.
I still remember your face when I told you I
hated school too.
It was like you thought someone was reading
your mind.
You would hate going to school and I was the
same. We both didn't want to be
at that place.
I think you knew this. I knew when to push
you, when not to push you.
I knew because it's how I would have felt
if I was you.
Some days you would just plonk yourself
down, exasperated. Done for the day.

All those new experiences for you, can't blame you.
I felt that so much!
When you were comfortable, you would ask so many questions about life.
I loved your curiosity about the bigger things. Another thing I would relate to.
The odds are highly unlikely, but if you ever somehow find this book and read this poem, on this page.
I could relate to you. The anxiety, hating failure, the hoodie, not wanting to be at school, the exasperation.
I hope you are doing well. I hope you have found some sort of peace.
From, Mister J.

Enjoying the Simple Things

EARLY MORNING

The early morning silence was blissful and
calming
chirping birds sung their heart out in the
trees, oh how charming.
The gentle breeze on my face helped to wake
me up
as I walked down my street with heavy eyes.
A school zone came into my path
it was a mad rush of students walking to
school breathing deep sighs
Everyone was walking with a purpose –
to get to school, some were walking slowly
without a care
Car engines and horns filled the air

The strong scents and fumes of cars and
buses passing by hit me in the face
and disappeared behind the smell of rain
My surroundings became peaceful again
Suddenly the rushed feeling faded away
instantly
The trees along the footpath swayed with
the wind
I looked above and found the sky had been
dimmed
The steam from my breathing became visible
like a chimney
Pitter Patter Pitter Patter
Drops of rain fell and spattered
My glasses became useless; they looked like
a car windshield
It was time to return home, as I was chilled.

Take Me Back

Sit on this motorcycle of black
and faded blue
Close your eyes, allow it to take you back
Back to when this bike was brand new
In 1960, this bike needs a rider with a knack
The engine roars as it leaves the garage
Gliding on the road
through meadows and hills
The vibrating tank gives a weird massage
Speeding and weaving –
testing the limits for thrills
The hot sun reflects off the shiny metal frame
The wheels spin faster as the speed increases

Passing through cities and towns,
for a rider there is no aim
Only quick stops to give it a splash of fuel
or the engine ceases
Open your eyes, see that this bike
has many stories of old
As it sits, rusted in the dark, realise that
nonliving things also become old.

THROWAWAY
SOCIETY

THE LIFE OF A CAR

I have been in this yard as long as
I can remember
Some stay and some go,
there is always leaving
Surrounded by gates, for fear of men thieving
Yet I am tucked away in the corner,
waiting for a peek
Amongst the others, some new,
some antique
Life as a man's possession
or something he is storing
Seems dull and boring, although they keep
our engine roaring

Whether it be new paint jobs, a wash,
mufflers or fenders
They look after and then sell us off
to strangers of every gender
In the end, it is not us they care about,
for it is the profit
I would be replaced in an instant if my
engine were to cough it
Humans are a throw away breed
and we cars are but doomed.

HEALTH

BEAST

Sounds are getting louder;
my eyes are becoming tight
My neck to head, every move makes
the sharp pain shoot
There's a beast inside and with my brain
it is in a fight
Medication won't help me,
this beast is a brute
Will I pass out? I just want to lie in bed
Lights are needles piercing my eyes
Every movement rattles my brain in my head

The beast twirls my brain, vomit is on the rise
My head is spinning out of control
The beast shuts down my body, it is weak
Face is melting, probably down to coal
I close my eyes, to rid this pain is what I seek
I force myself awake and for now I work in
dim lighting
What has caused this? Stress?
Oh, the joys of poetry writing.

FINDING
CONFIDENCE

Over Thinking

Let me begin with a shout out to dickheads
Let me make it clear for those with thick
heads
I'm thinking I'm back just like John Wick said
I was so hard on myself
always applying pressure
Told myself I was lesser
There was so much overthinking
That I was just over thinking
Over it
Got a bit of confidence now life is fun
I work so hard my boss said I am a gun
I said yeah but don't fire me
I'm rolling but it doesn't tyre me

Feeling like a whole new person
Jordan 2.0 a whole new version
Put myself out there and they're all lurking
Doing me so good and it seems to be
working
Eyes went from wetter to better, feeling
sharp like shredder
I'm just happy to tell
I'm finally out of my shell
I say I don't give a fuck but I'm also a
sensitive soul
Thanks to all who stuck with me
now we can roll
this life is a play, shitty people tend to
change roles
I'm no good at soccer but I've gotten all of
my goals
Checked them all off, now I need more
I now wonder what is in store.

4 A.M.
THOUGHTS

4 A.M.

4 a.m. it's late,
No one to bother me

4 a.m. it's late,
No expectations from anyone

4 a.m. it's late,
The world stops

4 a.m. it's late,
I can hear myself think

4 a.m. it's late,
Me time, me time

4 a.m. it's late,
Time to work
4 a.m. it's late,
Work on my writing

4 a.m. it's late,
Work on my hobbies

4 a.m. it's late,
Time to process the day

4 a.m. it's late,
Perfect.

INNER PEACE

INNER PEACE IN THE FORM OF LOVE, HARD WORK & HOBBIES (HAIKU SEQUENCE)

I have searched for this
This is my wife and my home
I've found inner peace.

My dreams do come true
I've dreamt of writing this book
Hard work and passion.

Focusing on these
Passions make me excited
Fun things to work on.

I WAS WRONG

I was wrong with my old way of thought
A kind of self-hate that was self-taught
For a long time, my degree
"It was a waste of money" I would plea
I didn't think I needed to study
English & Creative Writing
I kept on fighting
Until I wrote this book
Suddenly, it was all worth it,
all the tears it took
Dreams do come true
It just takes some belief from you
I know "How cliché"
But this is true, what I say

I was totally wrong
I have found inner peace, I finally belong
I was so angry, I didn't have to be
Now I am not and totally free.

About the Author

Creative video content creator and writer, Jordan Jurkowski is the author of *4 A.M. Thoughts*, capturing an insight into depression and anxiety, love, loss, and many other aspects of life.

After witnessing his grandfather, Gerald Carmody, publish his own book, Jordan has aspired to write his very own.

He obtained a Bachelor of Arts degree, majoring in English and Creative Writing, through The University of South Australia.

Jordan lives in Adelaide with his wife.